Backpacking Essentials
A quick start guide to backpacking light for beginners

PAUL GREENE

ISBN: 150878308X
ISBN-13: 978-1508783084

"Thousands of tired, nerve-shaken, over-civilized people are beginning to find out going to the mountains is going home; that wilderness is a necessity..."— John Muir

CONTENTS

1 INTRODUCTION

Last Morning- Sierra Backpacking. Photo by Scrubhiker

Good weather is the perfect time to get out into the great outdoors while hiking through the forest or wilderness in your area. It's exciting to leave the busy world behind and head off into the sunset to become one with nature—or something like that.

Getting away from it all is therapeutic and getting exercise while exploring areas of the earth that you have never seen before is like icing on the cake. It's time to grab your backpack and head out for a day of fun and adventure.

Before you begin cramming your pack full of this and that (we're sure those hardcover books will come in handy should you encounter a bear), you need to read this to determine just what it is you need to be packing in your backpack. Quite frankly, your life may just depend on it.

The lighter your pack, the easier you can move and the less strain you will be putting on your body. By definition backpacking light is when the weight of your backpack, including the items that it is carrying, is around 20lbs or less. The three main culprits that stack on the weight will be your sleeping gear, shelter and of course the weight of the backpack on its own. Shave down the weight of these guys and you will be well on your way to carrying a lighter load. The less you carry, the more energy you have to devote to enjoying your hike.

Speaking of which...hiking is great, but it can be dangerous if you are not properly equipped. Mother Nature can be fickle and you'll want to be prepared to ride out a storm, deal with a twisted ankle or becoming lost. Knowing what to do and having the gear to do it can mean the difference between life and death. We'll cover this and other beginner tips for backpacking light in the pages that follow.

Ready to get started? See you in chapter one.

2 SAFETY & FIRST-AID

El Calafate, Argentina, Patagonia. Photo by Douglas Scortegagna

Your safety is the most important concern you have when you head out on a backpacking trip. Your gear is secondary. All the gear in the world will not help you if you hike right out into unsafe conditions that even the most experienced hiker would struggle to deal with.

You're intelligent enough to know that in many areas where people like to backpack into, cell phone service is spotty. You won't be able to call 911 and wait behind a tree for the cavalry to come swooping in to save you with lights and sirens blaring within a matter of minutes. Frankly speaking, your best bet is to avoid unsafe situations where possible.

Here are some tips to do just that.

Check the weather in the area and pay attention to the forecast. If you are planning an overnight trip, check what the temperatures are supposed to be at night and for the next day. If the weather is inclement, postpone your trip. Heading off in a snowstorm or dangerous lightning storm not only risks your life, but the lives of those who will be forced to try and rescue you.

Don't hike alone. You should always head out with at least one other person. The more the merrier! Make it an adventure with several of your friends.

Leave a map of where you will be and what time you expect to return with a trusted, responsible person. If you are not back at a certain time, the person can alert the authorities that you are in trouble and send them to the right spot indicated on the map you left.

Don't start your hike as if you are in a race. Running through unchartered territory is dangerous for your physical safety as well as your endurance. By lunchtime, you will be beat and dragging your feet. If you have identified a certain point on your map to stay the night, you will struggle to make it there if you've exhausted your energy early on.

It goes without saying that being safe when you head into the wilderness will make your trip much more enjoyable. You won't have to be constantly worrying about the weather and whether or not anybody knows where you are. You will be able to focus on your surroundings and truly enjoy yourself.

First Aid Kit Basics

Your first aid kit is of the utmost importance and should be one of the first things into your backpack. There are too many scrape ups that can turn into serious injuries if not tended promptly with an adequate first aid kit.

With that said, it isn't necessary to carry around one of those tackle box-style first aid kits, but you will need to pack a kit designed specifically for backpackers or create your own. The kit should weigh less than 2 pounds or thereabouts and fit neatly into your backpack.

Every hiker should have their own kit. Do not rely on the idea that cautious John has one so I don't need one. That is a dangerous way to think, because what if you get separated from John? Sure, he'll be fine but what about you?

If you don't want to purchase one of the ready-made kits, use the following list to pack your own kit. Use a large Ziploc bag to store your items in. Place that bag inside a zipper pouch or as is inside your backpack. The Ziploc bag will give you some protection from moisture.

> 3 to 4 bandages from each size, small, medium and large
> Butterfly bandage closures—at least 2
> ACE bandage
> 2 2x2 gauze pads and 2 4x4 gauze pads
> Antibiotic cream—these are available in small single-use packs that take up very little room in your kit
> Medical tape
> Antiseptic wipes
> Moleskin for blisters
> Antihistamine tablets (Benadryl)
> Pain relievers (Advil, Tylenol)
> Pepto Bismol tablets or something similar
> Powdered electrolyte mix
> Calamine lotion or hydrocortisone

If you have any medical conditions, like diabetes or a severe allergy, you will need to pack some glucose tablets or insulin and an EpiPen. This kit is very basic and tailored towards those who will be backpacking for a short period.

Blisters on your feet can become a huge concern. You need to take care of your feet so you can walk back to safety. Blisters that are left untended grow and risk becoming infected; just as a minor cut can quickly become infected if not treated right away. You may not think twice about a cut on your leg in your daily life, but when you are in the outdoors you have to think about the bugs that will see your open wound as an invitation. Clean it and cover it right away.

Oh, and about those bugs? Bugs and biting insects are a part of the great outdoors. Unfortunately itching can lead to a break in the skin, which can lead to an infection. Pack along hydrocortisone or calamine lotion to alleviate the itching and potentially avoid a serious problem.

Do not get carried away with your first aid kit. The above list is adequate for a day or two out in nature. You need to keep your pack as light as possible and carrying around a bunch of extra medical supplies will only serve to hinder you and possibly cause an accident by trying to carry a heavier than necessary backpack.

3 NAVIGATION

Backpacking. Photo by [Matthias Ripp](#)

The next statement may seem obvious but it has been the tragic demise of many who have failed to adhere to it. You absolutely have to know where you are going so you can find your way back. Why? There are no street signs or telltale buildings that will help lead you in the right direction.

Once you are out in nature, things start to look the same. Trees, rock formations and other landmarks blend together and it doesn't take long before you get lost. It isn't feasible to tie a strip of cloth on brush and trees in an attempt to find your way back and for obvious reasons breadcrumb trails are not a good idea either. You need a good navigation system, especially if your inner sense of direction is somewhat lacking.

As a society, we have become very reliant upon our GPS systems in our cars and on our phones. We have signs directing us on the road, in large office buildings and even in the grocery store. It is a bit of a shock to get out into nature and realize you are totally on your own.

Ideally, you will want to carry at least **2 ways to navigate**.

GPS

As you have probably discovered in the past, GPS is not always available in certain areas. Ironically, remote areas are rarely covered by the satellites needed to run your GPS unit. So, although those little gadgets are extremely handy and fairly easy to use, you need a backup plan that doesn't require any technology.

Map

You need to have a map, preferably a topographical one, of the area in which you will be backpacking in. Topographical maps will help you identify the best path to take. The maps show different elevations as well as vegetation in the area. You don't want to try and walk over a rocky ridge if there is a nice, grassy meadow.

Study your map before you ever head out. Get a good feel of the landscaping so you can plot your course beforehand. This will make it much easier for you to reach your destination. It is also a good idea to put your map in a sealed plastic bag, just in case you encounter rain. You don't want your only navigation tool to get wet and blur.

Compass

A compass is old school, but reliable. You don't have to rely on satellites or anything that takes batteries. Compasses are fairly easy to use, but there is a bit of a learning curve. Take the time to learn how to hold a compass in order for it to get an accurate reading. Buy a good quality compass. Cheap compasses are rarely accurate and tend to bounce all over the place. A good compass is an investment worth making. Clip your compass onto the outside of your backpack or on a belt loop for quick access.

Ranger Beads

This method of navigating is for survival enthusiasts who like a bit of a challenge. You can use Ranger beads or what are technically known as Pace Count beads, in combination with your compass to give you an idea of how far you have walked. If you know you need to walk 8 miles, but the terrain looks all the same, having a reference tool can be very helpful.

Essentially, the beads hang on a leather string from your pack. You will need to count how many paces it takes for you to cover 100 meters. The average person will take 50 steps to cover that distance. Every 50 steps, you would slide a bead down, indicating you have covered 100 meters. There are about 1600 meters in a mile. While this method isn't exactly conducive to keeping a conversation going and counting your steps at the same time, it is effective and serves as an excellent backup plan to a GPS device.

4 SHOES & CLOTHING

Backpacking Incan Trail - Machu Picchu Peru. Photo by
fortherock

When you are out in nature, fashion should be
the last thing on your mind. Of course you want
to look good, but now is not the time to choose

style over function. Your clothing and shoes are your only protection from the elements. You need to make every piece of clothing you put on count.

Shoes

The right footwear is crucial on a backpacking trip. Your feet are going to get used and abused and if you don't take steps to protect them, you are going to get abandoned. Feet are your number one concern.

Spend some time finding the right boots for the terrain you will be packing through. The most expensive pair of boots is not necessarily the best. However, cheap boots are likely of poor quality and that is something you must avoid. Weak seams will split and leave you with half a boot or a toe hanging out.

There are a few key points to consider when shopping for the ideal pair of boots.

> Water resistant
> Durability
> Weight
> Warmth
> Comfort
> Support
> Terrain design

Do not walk into a store and assume that since you are a size 10 shoe, you need a pair of size 10 boots. You need to try on a pair of boots with the socks you will wear while backpacking. Winter time requires heavy wool socks and summer packing will require lightweight, moisture-wicking socks.

Next, you need to buy boots based on where you will be packing. If you are going to be trekking over rocky ridges and paths that are non-existent, you need a solid pair of rough-trail boots that provide ankle support.

If you are going to be traveling a well-maintained path, you can opt for a lighter pair of trail boots. Mountaineering boots are for those folks who are half mountain goat and love scrambling up rocky hillsides in cold weather. The boots provide some insulation, few seams (abundant seams can rub the feet and cause blisters), ankle support and plenty of traction.

Do not buy a boot that feels a little tight in the toe area with the hopes of breaking it in. To do that, you are sacrificing your feet and will most certainly have blisters. Buy a pair of boots that feels good from the get go.

Clothing

The key to dressing for a day or weekend backpacking trip is layers. You need a layer for warmth and you need a layer for protection from the elements. The amount you carry can vary depending on the length of your trip so we'll iron out the basic items you need at minimum to prevent your carrying extra weight. Your choice of layers will depend on the time of year and the weather in which you will be backpacking in.

If it is wet with a chance of rain or snow, your outer layer needs to be water repellant. Passing rain is always a possibility, especially in winter, fall and spring. Always be prepared. Getting wet could be more than just uncomfortable. It could put your life at risk if your body temperature drops. Summer backpacking trips require only a light jacket to ward off early morning and late night chills.

The second layer is all about insulating. This only applies to cool-weather backpacking trips. Fleece and wool are nice and toasty and will keep you warm. Don't forget to keep your legs warm as well with a pair of insulated, water-proof pants in the winter.

Now, you may not think twice about what underwear you put on in the morning, but if you are headed out backpacking, you need to. You need underwear that will keep you dry. Walking will make you sweat and the last thing you want to be dealing with is any chafing. Almost any material will do just fine. However, there is one absolute no-no—NO COTTON! Cotton retains moisture and any sweat you produce will be absorbed by the cotton against your skin.

When choosing what to wear, go for pants and shirts with few seams. Ideally you will want to carry one moisture wicking short sleeve & one long sleeve shirt. Convertible pants save space and eliminate the need for packing both a pair of shorts and pants separately.

Your clothes should be loose-fitting, but not overly so. You don't want to become a human parachute. Choose light-colored long-sleeve shirts and pants—even in the summer. You need to protect your skin from the sun as well as keep ticks and other nasty insects from hitching a ride. Again cotton is not a good idea. It's a good idea to choose synthetic, lightweight fabrics. The only time cotton should ever be worn is in the desert when you need to stay damp to cool.

You don't have to spend a lot of money picking your backpacking outfit. Keep it simple and you will be much better off. Guess what? It doesn't even have to match!

Remember, you are going to be outside and there is a very strong possibility you will get dirty. If you have a favorite white shirt, think twice about putting it on for your outdoor adventure.

5 FIRE & LIGHT

Winter Backpacking. Photo by Joseph

The rule of thumb is you never, ever leave your house and head into nature without at least two ways of starting a fire. Fire is a lifesaver plain and simple and you cannot afford to be without it. We all appreciate being able to see our surroundings and fire does that for us. If we can't have fire, we need some kind of light at the very minimum. It is really a safety feature. If you can't see where you are going, you could trip and fall and end up with some grievous injury that puts your life at risk. There are not any street lights or light switches or bulbs that clap off and on when you need to see something. You have to bring your own. Period.

Light

Let's deal with light first. Fortunately, we are lucky we don't have to rely on fire to see. Flashlights are available in various sizes that make them easy to pack along without packing along several pounds of bulk.

Ideally, you will want to choose an LED flashlight. They are extremely compact. Light weight and bright. When possible, choose an LED that does not require typical batteries. Watch batteries are often used to power some of the more compact lights. They last for hours on end and weigh under a pound.

Always include a headlamp as part of your lighting gear. The flashlights are attached to a band that is worn around your head. This leaves your hands free to carry your water, compass or whatever else.

Solar powered flashlights are incredibly handy as well, especially if you are planning an extended trip. You can attach the solar panel to the outside of your pack so it gets plenty of sun while you are trekking. You won't have to worry about running out of batteries or packing along a heavy extra package of batteries.

However, it must be said that if you are traveling in the rain or under particularly cloudy skies or a shaded environment, the solar rays may not be enough to recharge your flashlight. Always have a compact battery-powered flashlight as a backup.

Fire

If you are staying overnight in the outdoors, a fire is pretty much a requirement. However, even if you are not planning on staying out all night in the wilderness, you need to be prepared to do so just in case.

A fire provides warmth, light, a way to heat food and can deter animals and bugs. There are plenty of different ways to start a fire. Each of them require very little space in your pack and are incredibly lightweight. Pick at least two items from the list and stow them away in an outer pocket of your pack for easy access.

Waterproof matches
Lighter
Flint rod
Magnesium stick

All of these things are great for creating that spark you need to get a fire going, but if it is dark, wet or the ground is covered in snow, it is helpful to have the makings of a tinder bundle in your backpack as well. A tinder bundle is the dry stuff you need to start a fire. The following are a few things you can stow away in your backpack to help you start a fire in tough conditions.

Save the lint from your dryer screen and store in a sandwich bag

Collect dried moss from trees as you hike through forested areas

Collect and store dry grass—at least a sandwich bag full

Wipe Vaseline on a few cotton balls and store in an old pill container or sandwich bag

Shred an old bill and put the paper shreds in a sandwich bag

Keep your fire-starting materials somewhere close to the top of your pack or in an outside pocket. Chances are when you need to start a fire it will be dark or close to it. You want to be able to get the gear without rifling through your pack and spilling out all the contents. Keep your fire-starting gear all together. It is helpful to keep the items in a stuff sack so you can grab one bag and make your fire.

6 SKIN CARE & TOILETRIES

Backpacking Christmas Eve. Photo by Joseph

Your skin is a vital part of your protection. That's why you'll want to do everything possible to protect it from cuts, bites, burns and scrapes. One little cut is all it takes to throw a major wrench into your backpacking adventure.

As was mentioned in the clothing section, it is a good idea to cover as much skin as possible with long pants and long sleeves. Your face, ears and scalp also need some protection. Always wear sunscreen when you are outdoors, whether it is mildly cloudy or not.

Wearing a wide brimmed hat will protect your ears, the back of your neck and your scalp in warm weather. In cool weather, you should wear a hat with ear coverings or a pair of ear muffs to keep your ears warm. Why? Your body heat escapes via your head. This is important to remember for cool and warm weather expeditions. Choose a light, airy hat in the summer and a warm hat for cool weather.

Chapstick is necessary to keep your lips from drying and cracking in cool or warm weather. Keep a couple tubes with you at all times. If you have ever had to go without chapstick when you really needed it, you know it can make the difference between being comfortable and being absolutely miserable.

If you are going to be doing any climbing, pack sturdy gloves to protect your hands. Typically, backpacking doesn't involve any rock climbing, but if you are in rough terrain, you may need to climb over rocks or downed trees. Don't risk getting a cut.

You need to protect your skin from insects that will love to feast on you. It is a part of the great outdoors and there is no getting away from mosquitoes, ticks and other biting bugs. Have a good supply of bug repellant on hand. Many mosquitoes carry nasty diseases that can make you deathly ill. Cover up your skin and spray your clothing with bug repellant for added protection.

Chafing is always a potential problem when you are doing any kind of physical activity. Wearing the right clothing can help, but there are still times when your skin will rub repetitively against your clothing and become chafed. Avoid chafing by sprinkling powder in areas prone to chafing.

Groin area
Under your arms
Elbow area
Back of the knees
Waistband
Neck area where pack shoulder straps rub

Make sure to keep these areas dry at all times. If you feel yourself sweating, use a bandana or other cloth to pat away the sweat.

Toiletries

Just because you are in the great outdoors, you don't want to forego all personal hygiene duties. You are likely going to be with a few other people (if you say no, go back and read the safety chapter) and you don't want them running away in horror. You need to be able to take care of some of the basics in order to stay healthy and avoid those chafing issues that were mentioned above.

The following list of items is easy and lightweight to toss in your pack.

Toothbrush and toothpaste
Deodorant/antiperspirant
Soap
Toilet paper
Brush
Small shovel for digging a hole for bathroom needs
Small towel
Feminine hygiene products (these can double as other needs—tampons make excellent tinder bundle material and sanitary pads are excellent first aid for bleeding wounds)

Nature will call while you are outdoors. It is important to be responsible and practice good stewardship while you are out and about. When you need to use the restroom, dig a small hole at least 100 feet away from any bodies of water. After you have taken care of business, fill the hole in and put a rock or log over the top to deter animals from getting too curious.

While body odor isn't really that big of a deal when you are backpacking, it can make you feel uncomfortable. The idea is to enjoy yourself and if that means not stinking, then take along the necessary tools to prevent that from happening. You don't want to risk getting a toothache when you can't run to the dentist so oral hygiene is a must. A quick brush will keep your teeth clean and your mouth feeling fresh! If you are out in the wilderness with your significant other, you want to have fresh breath for those romantic kisses under the stars! Go ahead, roll your eyes.

7 FOOD & WATER

China Backpacking Trip. Photo by fortherock

We are living beings. Therefore, we need food and water to survive. When you are backpacking, you are expending a lot of calories and energy. You need to replenish the energy by eating food and you absolutely must continue to drink to stay hydrated. When it comes down to food and water, water is always your priority. You can get by on a few energy bars and ready-to-eat food rations, but you have to have a steady supply of water.

You need at least a gallon a day to stay hydrated. If it is hot outside and you are sweating a great deal, you may need up to two gallons of water per day. That isn't exactly convenient to carry. We are going to discuss your options for water first and then we will discuss food.

Water

Because you cannot possibly carry 2 gallons of water with you, you need to have a way to clean water you do find. When you head out on your trip, you will want to start with a minimum of one full water bottle, but two would be best. Stick them on each side of your pack to help balance the weight. You will need to pack at least one method to clean water you do find. You can reuse the water bottle you started with to hold the water. Choose one of the following methods of purifying water to pack with you.

Filtering straw

Purification tablets

Water bottle with built in filter

Portable filtering system

When you come across a stream, flowing river or a shallow creek, take the time to fill up one of your bottles. Purification can take anywhere from 15 minutes to an hour. While you are walking, the purification method will do its thing so you always have fresh water available.

Never, ever drink water without purifying it!

No matter how clear and gorgeous a mountain stream looks, it is likely harboring a whole host of dangerous, potentially deadly bacteria and viruses.

Food

You will need to pack a few energy bars for your excursion into nature. Energy bars are packed with the calories, protein, vitamins and minerals you need to keep going. They are super convenient and easy to eat on the go. They make great meals if you only plan on backpacking for the day. If you plan on spending several days in the wilderness, you are going to need a little more sustenance.

Freeze-dried foods make excellent meals and are easy to toss into your backpack. They do require water to rehydrate so keep this in mind when you are rationing your water. If you are able to set up camp close to a body of water, you will be just fine.

Jerky is a backpacker's best friend. It is tasty, full of protein and requires no preparation to eat. Choose jerky that isn't extra salty. You don't want to dehydrate yourself.

Trail mix is another good friend of the backpacking bunch. An assortment of nuts will give you the protein you need to keep your body going. You need protein for muscle health and energy.

Salami and aged cheeses are welcome additions to any backpack. They provide sustenance and are full of flavor. Sitting under a tree and enjoying some meat and cheese is the perfect end to a long day on the trail.

Always pack extra energy bars, trail mix and jerky when you head out, even if you don't plan on staying the night outdoors. You must always be prepared for emergencies that make it impossible for you to get back home as planned. You will also be surprised at how hungry you get after backpacking. It takes a lot of energy and calories.

8 PUTTING IT ALL TOGETHER

Backpacking Overnight. Photo by Joseph

Now that you know everything you need to put in your backpack, you need to know some tips and tricks to help make it all work. You don't want to be weighed down with a 40-pound pack that is lopsided, bulky and just a real nuisance to pack around. It can actually be a health hazard. Excess weight that isn't proportioned correctly across your back and hips can leave you unbalanced and cause a trip and fall. These 5 tips will help you make the most out of the space in your pack.

1-Pack things you need the most in the side pockets of your pack. Invest in MOLLE clips to save space by hanging gear off your backpack. Things like your flashlight, compass and a brightly colored bandana (for signaling just in case you get separated from your group) can all be placed on the outside of your pack.

2-Use a water bottle holder that attaches to your belt to keep your water easily accessible while freeing up space in your pack.

3-Use stuff sacks to keep like gear together. Your energy bars and food can be stored in one, while fire making supplies in another. Clear bags are best so you can see what it is you need.

4-Pack the bag so the heaviest gear i.e. coat and food are in the center of your back when the pack is on. Pack lighter stuff around it with the least used gear, like toiletries, on the bottom.

5-Keep the pack light enough so that it doesn't hurt your back or shoulders. Wear it around your yard a few cycles to test out the feel. If you feel it is too heavy, reevaluate your supplies and start removing things that are not essential.

Tackling the Big 3:

Backpacks

Generally speaking, the larger your backpack, the heavier it is going to be. This is why for those backpacking light, it is important to consider the length of your trip when deciding which backpack to carry. Carrying a backpack with a volume of 80 liters designed for longer trips when you are only going to be out for 1-2 days may not be the most practical choice if your goal is to cut back on the weight. Sporting goods retailers often categorize backpack volume by the duration of the trip which can make it easier when shopping for your pack. Ideally, for backpacking light, the base weight of your backpack should be 4lbs or less.

Sleeping Gear

A **water repellent** down sleeping bag provides greater insulation and packs less weight than your everyday synthetic model. Hammocks work great when weather permits and if sleeping pads are a must opt for one of the many lightweight options (many weigh in under one pound) available in the market. Even going from a full length sleeping pad to a ¾ length is enough to shave off some bulk.

Shelter

Let's face it. Tents can be very heavy and bulky items when they want to be. To save on weight you will want to go with an ultra-light tent; many of which weigh in at less than 3.5lbs. If less is more epitomizes your outdoor style, a tarp and rope will do just the trick to keep your head covered and your pack light.

Emergency Numbers

Although you want to abandon your busy life for a completely natural day in the woods, you need to have your cell phone with you along with a list of emergency numbers—just in case. You never know when you or a member of your party may suffer some injury or you come across something the authorities need to be aware of.

Forest service
Local Sheriff's
Local hospital
Animal control
Your next of kin i.e. spouse, parents, sister or whoever should be called in case of emergency
911
Your primary care doctor

In case you are injured and emergency personnel need to make calls for you, program these numbers into the ICE section of your cell phone address book. EMS workers are familiar with these and can quickly make notifications without trying to get the information from you.

9 A WORD ON HIKING STICKS

My trusty hiking stick. Photo by Sheila Sund

You don't really need to depend on a walking stick during your backpacking excursion however it's easy to see the benefits of one when you find yourself in need of additional support.

It is likely that you have witnessed backpackers carrying long, strong sticks in their hands. Why? A walking stick can assist a great deal in reducing your leg work. It enables you to save a great amount of strength due to the fact that a stick functions like an extra leg to support your weight.

Besides assisting your stability, a backpacking stick can also be beneficial in providing you a tool that's useful in your surroundings. For instance, you are able to use your backpacking staff to evaluate the depth of the stream without getting your arms or feet drenched in it. You can also move brush and plants apart easier to forge a path than clearing them with your hands.

Making use of a backpacking stick or two carries plenty of rewards for you. It could even save your life from an unwelcome animal in the woodlands or from falling. In many cases, you may not know what is waiting for you throughout the hike; even professional backpackers understand this perfectly. Therefore, it's definitely important that you carry something with you which is adaptable and can potentially save you from deadly situations.

The common rule of thumb when selecting a stick for hiking is to select the appropriate weight and height of your stick. Always purchase a backpacking stick which is 6 inches higher than your shoulder. This will provide you with sufficient length to make use of it for various functions. This will also provide you with a studier hold around the stick, giving a more solid grounding on an alpine trek. The weight on the other hand should be one that is most comfortable for you. From moderate to light, outdoor gear suppliers carry a variety of backpacking sticks which are ideal for every kind of hiker.

10 TIPS FOR BACKPACKING IN ALASKA

Denali National Park, Alaska. Photo by Alaska Range2

For anyone who is near to Alaska, you can probably imagine the thrills that you will experience as soon as you step into its territory.

Known as one of the best states for sheltering great backpacking locations, Alaska is bound to make an impression on you with its immense land mass. Alaska flows 2300 kilometers from east to west as well as 1400 kilometers from north to south. In between, you're more likely than not to locate the perfect trail for you.

It's an opportunity to discover mountain tracks for every level of backpacking, from beginner to expert. Plus, the state guarantees you beautiful scenery from downhill passes up to the well-known Alaskan tundra.

Alaska provides among the most exceptional displays of wildlife and regardless of its unexpected rain showers, Alaska backpacking will delight you with its stunning misty hills.

Listed below are a few of the most well-known Alaska backpacking locations for each level of backpacker:

Anchorage Backpacking and Chugach Hills

Backpackers who enjoy snowboarding and mountain cycling will discover that Anchorage is an excellent location to travel. It provides kilometers of both multi-use trails and smooth, paved trails. One of the most common sites in South-Central Alaska is the Chugach National Forest and Chugach State Park.

If forest bushwhacking is your style, head to Kenai Peninsula where trails ranging from snow-clad hills to meadows and sub-alpine ponds await you.

Seward Backpacking

Generally accessed via boat, along with the only road-obtainable spot via Exit Glacier, Kenai Fjords National Park provides excellent hiking trails for backpackers and the daring spirits of cross-country skiers. However before heading out, take note of the crevasses located on topographic charts which should be avoided for safety reasons.

In the event of challenges or an emergency situation, you can find help at the headquarters located outside Seward, a four hour travel from Anchorage. Seward is a well-known vacation destination for backpackers and features untouched trails along with stores that provide services for backpacking, camping and fishing equipment.

Denali National Park

For anyone who is looking for wildlife sanctuaries, Denali National Park is an ideal destination. It is well-known for cross-country vacations, heli backpacking, backcountry and flightseeing. Denali National Park also features untouched areas and it provides backpacking excursions just beyond the entrance of the park for exploring the backcountry.

Bear in mind (no pun intended) that there are plenty of bears within this section of the state, so it is highly advisable that you master the key safety strategies to prevent you from becoming prone to attacks.

Chena State Recreation Spot

Selecting Fairbanks or a spot nearby it give you trails formulated for prolonged hikes and day backpacking. Along the way you will find huge stone towers, woodland country for backpacking, swimming spots for canoeists and strong stone walks for mountain backpackers.

There is a great deal that Alaska backpacking can provide and its size lends to extensive trails for virtually every kind of soul. Rangers are always available to assist you with on journey and recreation area headquarters are logically located to provide the best possible services to tourists.

11 TIPS FOR BACKPACKING IN CALIFORNIA

Yosemite Valley. Photo by Nina

When backpackers think about hiking in California, the first thought that usually enters their mind is Yosemite Valley. Exactly what could be so interesting about the Yosemite Valley that excites ambitious souls?

For starters, Yosemite Valley provides a spectacular elegance of waterfalls, stone structures, cliffs and forests. You will soon find that no matter how long you gaze at the rugged stone structures, there will always be a new discovery with each glance. The Tuolumne River, which flows from numerous Tuolumne Meadows, is another breathtaking site that will transport you to another world.

Yosemite National Park hosts glacier-carved valleys, accented with large monoliths, exceptional waterfalls, magnificent coves and curved domes. The National park was founded near the end of the 1800's as part of the preservation of the Sierra Nevada. The level varies from 2000 ft. - 13000 ft. which lends to impressive vistas, from natural stone structures to impressive waterfalls.

There are millions of guests in Yosemite National Park each year and almost every one of them comes to gaze at the beauty of the Half Dome. Some hike suggestively in the direction of the top, some venture halfway up the trail and then there are those brave enough to reach the top making it a special place for tenacious hikers.

The North Dome, in contrast, is the most popular hiking trail in California. Other destinations include the Sentinel Dome, the

Glacier Point and obviously the Valley Floor. The North Dome is close to Camp Curry over Royal Arches.

There are several hiking trails up North Dome, starting from short tracks to extensive range tracks -all of them sporting pretty impressive views.

The hike in direction of the peak of North Dome gives a spectacular view of the half Dome that appears to be so close, it seems as though you can reach out and touch it.

Sentinel Dome is among the popular brief hikes within the Yosemite Valley and one of the few that's not jam packed. The trail doesn't give the feeling of going up a steep incline as it's an easy trail and as you hike, your target destination is always in sight.

The hike up Yosemite Falls is probably the most challenging and complicated trail. For this reason, horses aren't permitted so don't expect to find smooth trodden grounds. It's a trail that will take time to hike and can be described as an ascending staircase, ever winding its way upward.

These are only three of the greatest sites within the Yosemite National Park and you will find that they are some of the greatest when it comes to California backpacking.

12 TIPS FOR BACKPACKING IN MONTANA

Montana Backpacking. Photo by cjnoof *non deriv*

Montana resonates the number one thing backpackers seek -mountains!

Listed here are some of the best sites for backpacking in Montana:

Glacier Country

In 1910, the Glacier National Park was officially recognized and here you will find around 200 ponds and 50 glaciers as well as waterfalls, great downhill meadows and marvelous deep woodlands.

Throughout Glacier Country are a few of the greatest locations that backpackers, fly-fisherman and mountaineers alike can appreciate.

Hoskins Lake

Greatest when hiked between May-October, Hoskins Lake is best accessed making use of a brief trail in direction of the mountains. Families and day backpackers would appreciate this brief journey which lasts just for ten minutes, unless of course you stop to take in vision before you. There are actually two lakes, one at a higher elevation and another located at the lower part of the trail. The lower one is most popular for fishing.

Fish Lakes Canyon

Beginning from an impressive location that leads to a five-sequence lakes; Fish Lakes Canyon features some of the most varied and stunning trails of Montana. For expert backpackers, Fish Lakes Canyon is typically an overnight stop with the exception of those who wish to stay and camp out. Nevertheless, for the majority of backpackers the trail requires about 12 hours to complete. However, if you decide on viewing just the first collection of lake chains on its own, it will be around an 8 hour hike.

Peterson Lake

If you would like to hike among mid-June till September, your ideal spot in Montana is Peterson Lake. It features a fantastic view of the Sweeney Canyon and a couple of other mountain highs, along with a spread of lakes located within the mountains.

Lion Creek Pass

For the expert backpackers who would like a challenging hike, the Lion Creek Pass creates the ideal environment.

Great Northern

This has been referred to as the previous railway, nevertheless even the title matches precisely the encounter that is waiting for you. A great off-trail track suited for expert backpackers that have the experience of higher mountains and those who wish to have a look at what makes the mountain country appealing to ambitious souls.

Gold West Country

Discovered amongst the Glacier country along with the Yellowstone National Park, Gold West Country contains several snow-topped mountains and valley side trails which are made even more stunning by its background.

Trask Lake

If you plan on traveling to Racetrack peak and would also like to encounter the peacefulness and satisfaction of lake angling, Trask Lake is among the best destinations for you.

Grayling Lake

Underneath the darkness of Sharp Mountain are three popular lakes. Ideal for average backpackers, Grayling Lake creates a twelve-kilometer breathtaking hike that is best throughout July-September.

Lake Louise

Among the primary hiking excursions, Lake Louise features exceptional possibilities for family vacations and impressive surroundings which led it to be known as a National Adventure Trail.

Yellowstone National Park

Founded throughout the late 1800's, Yellowstone National Park features breathtaking sights equally in the springtime and summer season. In addition, it contains various rivers and downhill lakes as well as geysers and mud cauldrons.

Amongst the most popular backpacking locations in Yellowstone National Park are Spanish Mountains and Ram shorn Lake that are world-popular for fishing outings and its soothing backcountry.

13 CONCLUSION

Vermilion Cliffs National Monument. Photo by Bureau of Land Management

Backpacking is an excellent way to get outdoors while getting exercise. It can be a fun and rewarding experience when you are prepared to spend some time outdoors. Don't take chances with your life by failing to prepare for the little eventualities that tend to happen in nature.

Have fun...

Oh, and don't forget to pack your camera so you can take lots of amazing pictures!

"WALK THE WEIGHT OFF: HOW TO JUMPSTART YOUR WEIGHT LOSS WITH THE SIMPLE STRAIN-FREE WALKING PROGRAM ANYONE CAN DO" PREVIEW

Most fitness enthusiasts and fitness experts advise those who would like to stay fit and healthy to try power walking to gain faster results. Power walking is a form of exercise which is highly recommended by thousands of doctors and fitness experts because of its many benefits. Aside from being a simple and enjoyable activity, power walking is something that you can do almost anywhere.

When performed correctly, power walking can melt away fats as quick as jogging, maybe even at a faster rate. It is also a healthy and safe exercise because it does not put too much force or strain on your joints. Did you know that the force of power walking is half the force required in jogging once you start to hit the ground? This means that you have better chances of reaching your fitness goals fast without dealing with injuries and soreness.

If you are interested in power walking, this book contains almost everything that you need to know about this popular form of exercise including its benefits, tips on how to do it right, warm up and cool down exercises, what to wear, and more.

Walking isn't an expensive exercise to do and we all can benefit no matter age we might be. If your goal is to bring down your high blood pressure, lower your cholesterol, lose weight, or just maintain your health, walking will help you to reach your goal. The only thing you need to ensure is that you have a good pair of walking shoes to help prevent injuries and make your experience a happy one.

The information offered in this book is enough to guide you as you begin your journey to fitness with the help of power walking. The tips mentioned here can also be applied whether you are still a beginner or an advanced power walking enthusiast. So, let's get started!

POWER WALKING AND ITS PROVEN BENEFITS

Power walking can be defined as a type of walking performed at an energetic and steady pace. It consists of brisk and wide footsteps and pronounced arm movements. Power walking is also recommended for those who are looking for a great alternative to jogging. It is considered as a low to moderate exercise regimen which can produce around sixty to eighty percent maximum heart rate. This means that it can provide numerous fitness and health benefits without being too hard on your joints and muscles.

Power walking also means walking at an increased pace. Armed with the right information and proper technique, turning casual walking into power walking will be easy. The good thing about this style of walking is that it is considered a low impact exercise that can help increase your body strength while also improving your cardiovascular health.

Power walking is one of the most natural workout plans anyone can have. Ideally you should walk an average of 10,000 steps a day. However most of us are only getting between 1,000 and 3,000. If you quickly run the numbers you can see this is a long way from 10,000. By increasing the amount of steps you take, the more calories you can burn and the healthier you'll feel.

Walking can aid in the prevention of many diseases including colon cancer and reduce stress as well as give you a healthier body that looks amazing and feels comfortable in whatever you choose to wear.

As you read the pages to follow, you may notice that power walking has many similarities to jogging. This exercise, like its counterpart involves pumping your arms and moving your legs at a higher intensity for maximum results. If you want to increase resistance and intensity, then you can use hand weights or weights that you can strap into your ankle or wrist. This will increase the speed and range of motion of your exercise while also generating more fitness benefits.

The Proven Benefits of Power Walking

1. Supports Effective Weight Management

One of the main reasons why power walking has become so popular today is its effectiveness in managing weight. It works out the muscles using exaggerated and intense movement of the feet and arms. This increases the amount of calories burned in each power walking session. You can expect to burn around 236 to 345 calories every hour if you walk briskly (preferably 4mph). Combined with a healthy and fat-free diet, power walking can improve your health while also ensuring that unwanted pounds are kept at bay.

2. Promotes Better Health

Incorporating a regular exercise into your daily routine can improve your health since it combats various illnesses and diseases. The easiest exercise that you can do on a regular basis is power walking. You can walk briskly to and from the grocery store, around the neighborhood, or to and from your office if it is close to your home.

Staying consistent with your power walking routine can reduce bad cholesterol while also increasing good cholesterol levels. Since it is a cardio exercise, you can also expect it to reduce high blood pressure and decrease your risk of suffering from serious health conditions such as Type 2 diabetes, stroke and cancer.

3. Eliminates Stress

If you power walk every day, then the stresses brought on by your daily tasks and responsibilities can be significantly reduced. A single power walking session can even help you redirect your concentration and focus, which is useful in effectively dealing with stressful situations and environments. This form of exercise is also an efficient means of getting more engaged in your own time and releasing tension.

It releases more endorphins which is also a major help in achieving a calmer state of mind and a more relaxed disposition. You will feel more refreshed and renewed if you allocate at least thirty minutes a day for power walking - away from your busy home and the hectic pace in your office.

4. Power Walking is not Time-consuming

Another benefit of power walking is that you do not need to spend too much time to prepare for the exercise. You can just slip into a pair of comfortable sneakers, head out the door, and walk around your neighborhood. You do not need to spend time fighting with traffic to visit a gym, only to realize that most of the gym equipment including the treadmill is already used.

You can already reap the benefits of this exercise even if you do it for only thirty minutes a day, five days a week. Do you have a hectic schedule? Then you can also break down the required 30-minute power walk into three (that would be around 3 10-minute sessions daily).

5. Promotes Better Sleep

Engaging in power walking also results in longer and better sleep. It allows you to use all your pent-up energy, so you do not have to worry about tossing or twitching from side to side once it is time to get to sleep. It ensures a better and more peaceful sleep not only because it is a healthy physical activity, but also because of its usefulness in improving your health, boosting your mental equanimity, self-esteem and eliminating stress.

6. Improves your Performance at Work and at Home

If you power walk, your upper and lower body strength are used, which is a huge help in strengthening your bones and muscles. It conditions your body which also results in better endurance to carry out your daily tasks and responsibilities. Power walking on a regular basis can even increase your ability to successfully complete challenging tasks such as lifting heavy objects. It also promotes better productivity, feelings of accomplishment and better sense of your own self.

Now that you are aware of how power walking can benefit you, it is time to learn how to do it correctly. Are you ready to start? Then continue reading...

EXPLORE MORE FROM THIS AUTHOR

Below you'll find some of my other books that are popular on Amazon and Kindle as well. Simply click on the link below to check it out. Alternatively, you can visit my author page on Amazon to see other work done by me.

Walk The Weight Off: How To Jumpstart Your Weight Loss With The Simple Strain-Free Walking Program Anyone Can Do

Increase Testosterone: A 30 min Guide to Boosting Your Testosterone Naturally, Starting Now

You can simply search for the titles on the Amazon website to find them.

Made in the USA
Las Vegas, NV
05 March 2024